Nova. Phoenix. Grace.

Nova. Phoenix. Grace.

by

LaTonya S. Mitchell

First Edition
Printed in the United States of America
Cover Design: Mia Marie Overgaard
Interior Design: Vanessa Mendozzi
Editor: Daniel Johnson

ISBN: 978-1-7330149-0-8

Contents

Dedication

For the loves of my life: Zaire and Zaria
Keep your voices strong, and make sure they're
heard — don't ever quiet them.

Acknowledgments

So! This is it! I am finally publishing my poetry book. I feel a bit exposed, but I know that I am not alone. My hope is that you get a positive experience out of it; so please enjoy. This is my official acknowledgments page, and I need to get this out to my interior designer, so let me get to acknowledging. I must thank first and foremost, my Father, Jesus Christ, for allowing me to create this art, and providing me with the provisions to do so. Thank you for being the ultimate Gentleman and loving me no matter what. As I always tell You, I'm continually striving to be less of me, and more of You. Thank you, thank you, thank you, thank you! Mommy, none of this — none of me would be possible without you. When you told me that you are my biggest fan, I knew that I could do it. Thank you for allowing me to come by your house at all hours of the day and night to use your computer to push all of this through. This reminds me to also thank Tinisha. Cousin, thank you for being such a great inspiration and accountability partner in life. Thank you for allowing this simple yet complex woman to polish her poems in the comfort of your home. Daddy, thank you for reminding me that my poems are a work of art, and that they must be shared. I love you. Melanie, thank you for listening and supporting me. I love you. Zaire and Zaria — you two are the absolute light of my life, and I must thank you for being so patient during all of this. Publishing this book is indeed a great accomplishment, but you two are my greatest creation — beautiful, moving, thriving and bright rays of light. Don't ever dim it. Thank you to my ultimate powerhouse of support, love, and inspiration: Jasmine, Zyon, Cassandra, Taneisha, Holli, Talia and the rest of my god children, Vickie, Rosita, Alicia, Deonna, Kemar, Danielle, Momma (Christine), Ashley, Alexandria, Kathy, Candace, Cookie, Sukari, Jacquice, Cedrick, Joseph, Natalie, Patricia, Marjorie, Leon, Lonzell, Kelcey, Alexander, Theresa, William, Felicia, Wilma, Karen, Toni, Gabriel, Robbia, Jacqueline, Michella, Louise, Tanisha, Keaon, Charles, Ricky, Vivian, Nia, Seddrea, Capri, Monica, Steve, Adrianna, Rhonda, Sue, Krisitin — anyone else not mentioned, please charge it to my mind and not my heart. You are loved and appreciated by me. I thank you too for the love and support. Be blessed.

Preface

Nova. Phoenix. Grace. is comprised of poetry that I have been writing since I was around 16 years old. My high school English teacher had introduced poetry to me, and I began to play with it. I had come to find that poetry was a way of expression and release for me. It quickly became a natural part of my life. The chapters within this book are separated into three stages; respectively:

Nova — a collection of some of my earlier poems. This chapter depicts my discovery of poetry and how I've used it to find myself within words, verbal expression, the world, and the people in my world and surrounding areas.

Phoenix — all about reflection, boldness, taboo topics, and rising above various hardships.

Grace — a reflection of the peace and refinement I've come to find within self, life, and the human experience — the journey of becoming whole.

Prologue

June 16, 2018

These words brought forward are of my own soul, spirit, heart, mind, and body. They were birthed through me. I pray that God and the universe guide them to the one destined for enlightenment, connection, questions, oneness, likeness, light, love, courage and understanding. Thank you for giving me the honor of being a part of your reading experience. Be blessed and free.

Nova

Longing

I desire to be clear
Free of this guilt and weight and struggle
Free of containment
To be lighter, freer
Graceful
Blades of grass prickling my skin
The ravine singing sweet nothings in my ear
Surrounded by leafless trees
An autumn night
Constellations and all their eminence above me
Dark and bright and wondrous
The things they've seen
The places they've traveled
Birds soaring through the sky
They're free like me

Time

Ticking
Steady moving
Ascending
Descending
Uncertain

Late and precise all at once
Impatient and judgmental
Yet unprejudiced and irrevocable

Punctual in its own order
Acquisitive when searched for

Comforting in the known
Soothing in dark journeys
Yet erratic and radical
Never timid

Controlling within itself
Uncontrollable in its freedom
Unfathomable in the unknown
Yet, we all need it...

Speechless

Your sweet face
Silkening words
Gestures of gratitude and empathy so eloquently
executed
Full of compassion and grace
Surging magnetism
Flaming and bright
A force so intense
My heart skips a beat twice
Tranquil is your touch
I cannot think
I cannot speak

Dear Music

Dear Music,
My love. You give me life. I will forever celebrate
you. You are the notes and blueprints to my soul.

Draft #1

Your eyes tell a story of something I have yet to experience

A force so dark, so deep and strong

It's pulling me in along with you

Stripped and unable to move

Words I cannot formulate

Emotions untapped

Limbs totally immobile

I'm shell-shocked

What is this?

A Hookup

Where's the hookup sites where people don't want to "hookup"?

Just swipe right, message, relate, and hookup?

Hookup and go to random places and see how they enlighten us.

Hookup and stare at the stars, contemplating all things past.

Hookup and read excerpts from our favorite literature and tell one another what they mean to us.

Hookup and explore a different part of this world, or another.

Why does it all have to be so sexualized?

New York

New York
New York
New York

Oh, how I wish and dream to become thee

Your nostalgic lights

Bustling nights

Shades of divine diversity

Freedom of individuality

I'm Brooklyn sometimes

I'm Detroit most of the time — with Harlem at the
edge of my pen

Writer's Block

Mind on full
Hands trembling
Mouth watering, ready to speak my heart's song

Don't know what to say or how to use the right
words

Mind titillated, being teased by my hand's caress
as I allow ink to collide with page

Hot
Cold

Ok — stop, go

Play my word's song

I'm stuck!

So many words, not enough time to formulate

It's an eruption

Your Photo

Your photo ignites some kind of unfamiliar passion
in me

A desire full of curiosity and certainty all at once

I'm taken aback

Willing to put in the time to unwind you

Decipher your code

Inside and out

My mind and intellect so aroused by you

A simple photo

Yet, I read so much of you

All of the beautiful hues of you

Yearning to caress, express

Mind — focused
Heart — steady
Body — yearning
Knees — weak

I'm in a place where my mind loses itself within my flesh and limbs

Heart — pacing
Fire burning core

I'm on a natural high
And you haven't even touched me yet

Better yet, don't

Just speak those slow, long, meaningful, genuine words that my tongue yearns to taste so that my body can let go

As I Look Into Your Eyes

As I look into your eyes,
I see what I've been searching for in love
What seems a million lifetimes

As I look into your eyes,
I realize that what I'm feeling could never be
explained in words — but expressed in the grat-
itude, loyalty, and eternal love and compassion I
have for you

As I look into your eyes,
My heart races, my body embraces every touch
from your hand as it calms my soul and reaches
the deepest depth of my heart

As I look into your eyes,
My emotions take control of every moment we share

As I look into your eyes,
I cry, because only your love could feel this good
— secure and real

As I look into your eyes,

I view who and where I am supposed to be — with you in eternity

As I look into your eyes,
Each time I am reminded once again just how much I love you

As I look into your eyes,
I see all that we have been through, and still the lowest tone of your voice and the swiftest touch of your hand sends my body, mind, and soul into pure bliss

As I look into your eyes,
I see that the love I once had for you hasn't changed one bit, and despite all that has happened, I'd do it all over again

As I look into your eyes,
I see just how much of a soul mate you are, and that I am you, you are me, and we are one...

Love Analogy

Love is 2 pain, for it may hurt

Love is 2 endure, for endurance is 2 bear, and bear is 2 strengthen

Love is 2 struggle, for it is required 2 strengthen love, unity, and trust

Love is 2 take chance, for love has no limits

Love is 2 battle, for its roads will not always be smooth

Love is 2 cry, for there will not always be a sunny sky

Love is 2 ensure, for it will never lie and always keeps its promise

Love is 2 embrace, for you must hold on 2 it or you will fall

Love is 2 care, for carelessness is not needed

Love is 2 be honest, for honesty is the key 2 everything

Love is 2 be loyal, for without loyalty, there is no love or trust

Love is 2 not question, for if love is there, there is no need 2 question

Love is 2 trust, for without trust, there is no stability

Love is 2 realize, for if you do not see it, you will
be cheated
Love is 2 accept — if you do not accept, why?
Love is 2 conceive, for love is 2 not only understand,
but visualize
Love is 2 know, even though it may take time
Love is 2 be patient, for patience is a virtue
Love is 2 infinity, for it will never end

And foremost…

Love is 2 you, for you are my love, and there is and
never will be any other

Trial and Error: Love's Ultimate Recipe

You can't miss or want something you won't allow into your life

Don't let 1, 2, 3, 4, 5, 6, 7, 8, 9, 10 bad experiences define your meaning of love

It's all about the discovery of actions and emotions

You have to learn to mix 'em up a bit to see what pleases your palate

You're simply seasoning up your meat, allowing it to marinate, and placing it in the oven for the ultimate dish!

Wait

I've never held your hand
I've never spoken your name
And yet, I wait for you

Anticipating your arrival (and sometimes not) to
capture my heart
And will all of my premature assumptions of you
away.

Are you kind?
Are you driven and focused?
Do you exude dominance and leadership?
Are you patient and unyielding?
A provider?
A goal pusher?
Game changer?
Paternal figure?

And ultimately, will you force me to let my guard
down?
Will you help me release my true self?
Because I'll need you to. I really will.

Learn me
Embrace me
Accept me
Enhance me
Lighten me
Love me
Desire me
Need me
Enlighten me

Be patient with me.
Because I'm hard.

Ambivalent

I have a desire to reach out to you
And if given the time allotted, I will use it wisely,
carefully, slowly,
With genuine, meaningful words and expressions
and elaborations

Nothing false
Nothing altered

Just an offer of friendship and growth

Don't shy away
Into your sheath;
Try not to shield me
I want to see you

Let's give us a fair chance at growth
And how we complement one another

This is no fairy tale —
Those don't exist
But I offer the chance to create one with you
Of our own territory

Strong and steady

Don't be timid

I am transparent
I am strong

Just a single person
Looking for plurality with you

In time
Just give me
Give us
The go!

Phoenix

The Thing She'd Never Say

He touched me
I didn't know it was wrong
Uncomfortable urges
Unknown feelings
Lost in the actions
Familial connections
Trying to do things you shouldn't have seen
No one can know
So it's wrong, right?
Passing through time
With one and then another
Crossing over
This isn't right

Twice Hurt, Twice Broken

Twice hurt
Twice broken

She should've been your princess
And you her queen

Stripped of support and guidance that should be
instilled constantly from the wake of life

Naturally yearning to be noticed and wanted by you

Yet, you look over her
Take her for granted
With guilt and a steel heart that only softens as you
show "love" when you see fit

But love has no on and off switch

She shared some of life's most intimate experiences
with you

Coming into life without permission through pain
and love

Creating and bringing in life with a love that was
falsely found

Twice hurt
Twice broken

You were her first
Twice
To love
To need
To depend on

She held on with a huge heart and hard love

At the beginning of life
And the turn of another

Twice hurt
Twice broken

Constantly praying that you would never leave her side
See her as your jewel
Someone you refused to live without
But instead
You live

And she dies everyday
From your constant abuse
Absence
In and out
Lost time
Unsaid words
False formalities
Unfair judgment
Harsh words
Lack of closure
And no true chances

Twice hurt
Twice broken

Her father
Her first love
Twice

Big Mouth

Don't ask me a question if you don't want me to answer it.

Don't tell me something if you don't want me to inquire further about it either.

I'm Full Ob Shit!?

My friend, my sister
I loved you
I trusted you
I confided in you…
But, *I'm* full of shit!?

I was there when you needed me (so I thought)
Late night convos
Last minute get-togethers
Graduations
Doctor's appointments
Candid texting
Baby showers, play dates, dinner dates
Man problems, abortions, STIs…
But, *I'm* full of shit!?

Somewhere I missed it
During my heartache
Hardship
Psychological and emotional imbalance
Breakdowns
Brokenness
Growing into my own

More was expected, I guess;
More was needed, I guess —
From us both

I valued our friendship
Sister-ship
Memories
Feelings
Thoughts

Does it matter that you used my resilience under
pressure as a compass and comparison for your
come up?
Was it worth it while you conspired against me in
order for you to feel superior?

Wait!
Right...*I'm* full of shit!

Happy Father's Day

She said that when she finally had a child, the father would be great, and his name would be on the birth certificate

The child got the latter

To have the man that deposited the seed take part in a child's makeup, their being, is so damn critical, vital

For a solid base
For a solid foundation
For a solid upbringing
For support
For courage
For love
For consistency
For example
For acknowledgment

But you'd rather be a frivolous man

And that makes you a terrible father

Messenger

My vagina flinched when I saw you
So I made that call
Laid that pipe
Destroyed that notion
Continued my day
Phone hasn't stopped ringing

A Virgo

Your foreign car
Six-figure income
Mini mansion
Amazing ambition and work ethic
750 credit score
American Express, Black status

And yet, you can't handle the realities of life

Benefits of Music

Music has given me more love, loyalty, provision, passion, and orgasms (mental, physical, and spiritual) than a man ever has!

Connect The Dots

You can't have a connection with someone if you don't have a solid connection with yourself.

Growth

When you fear yourself

You're on the brink of growth

Stop standing on its neck

Let it go

Let it breathe

Don't let the remnants of an old life and habits bind
its resurgence

Inception of Artistry

Some of the greatest pieces were created in pain and darkness

Conscious of the creation or not

Like diamonds formed under pressure

Only a true artist will understand this

Friend Zone Promotion

I catch myself wanting to do something with you all
the time —

Like tell you about my day

Model a pair of jeans I'm not quite sure if I look
good in

Talk constantly

Look in your eyes and smile at you

Kiss your lips

Slip up and call you "girl" while having a
conversation

Make love all night

Watch a stupid movie

Debate about life and what makes people do the
things they do

Fuck you

Argue

Cry on your shoulder and be held by you

Talk about work

Share joyous occasions

Build something as simple as a sandwich, and as big as a home

You scare me

I like that

It lets me know that what we have is genuine

And that I can trust it

I can trust you

With my heart

How does one release their heart to another

With hopes that they'll care for it tenderly, gently,
lovingly, and proudly?

The End of Life as We Know It

Your image exposed me
Stripped me

I looked into your eyes
My storm silenced
I stood at a standstill
Full of familiarity
You saw me

Simple thoughts of you
I'm smiling
Blushing
Blooming on the inside

My heart
My world
Put at ease

Overwhelmed with certainty
Cradled in your love's embrace
I saw you
I see us

At that very mystifying moment
I knew
I just knew
I would love you from then on
Forever

You're the keeper
Guardian of my heart

It took me years to fully prepare for what you've
had unyielding faith in:
Us

Now, all I think about are ways to reassure you that
I'm the one you need

Fear
Circumstance
Time
Life
Trials
Tribulations
Blindness
Stupidity
Ignorance

Lessons in love
Busy workin' on me

These things are no longer a concern

You never gave up
Neither did my heart

You have strengthened my hope, desire, and drive
to live life beyond what I have thus far
To move forward
Embrace love, life, and faith with you

And now, all I need to know is…
Will you let me?

Rain

Rain. Moist.
Silence. Soft.
Thunder. Warmth.

Thoughts of you fall in between.

To feel you
Connect with you
In the most intimate display that you and I know of

Your skin,
Your lips,
My neck.

Hands so strong
Right beneath me;
My thighs so ready.

Spine tingling,
Silkening intensity —
Boldness!
Your boldness.
Yes! Your boldness.

Plunge into me.

Wait!

Don't ease away.
Come back.
Slow. Deeper.
Steady. Arching.
Nerves begging for more,

Deep dark eyes pulling me in,
Wanting to stay a while longer,
Stripping each other of everything but submission.
Hearts wrapped in silk,
Body caught between clouds and your seductive
rapture,
Hips rolling with the waves your ocean releases,

Breathing deep,
Release caught in my throat.
Tight,
Creamy,
Sweet pleasure.

Farthest limbs in search of something to grasp.

The most intense of pleasures.
Gasping…
Thunder cracks!

Humanity: The Greatest Wonder In The Universe

I think I was a little bit of everybody in my past lives

I understand and relate to it all, collectively —

A pharaoh in ancient Egypt with all her romantic cohorts, her republic, her insight and values

A woman of Rapa Nui with a keen eye and survivalist heart

An Amazonian woman who hunted for food amongst her magnificent forest

An Englishman born of privilege, sailing the seas and afraid of not pleasing his demanding father with his "discoveries"

A female slave being used as a breeder

An elderly, cancer-stricken man who lives long enough to walk his daughter down the aisle

A man of African descent who is the first to graduate

from college, summa cum laude

A single mother sacrificing quality of life for survival

A Holocaust survivor who stresses the importance of self-identity, overcoming barriers, and being self-sufficient

A woman in remission after chemo

A deaf man given treatment, able to hear his wife's voice for the very first time

An astronaut taking their first mission into space and seeing the wider universe

A California dreamer surfing Mavericks

A young girl embracing her sexuality

A young boy taking a ride on a fire truck

A black woman who fell in love with a white man

A six-month-old baby being so tickled with laughter

that their cheeks turn red

The woman who declares that we are all of one human race with majestic souls, endless significance, and meaning!

It's the little big experiences and accomplishments that make us profound...even in all our darkness... and "differences"

Embrace them all now!

Summer's Eve

Smiling
Swinging
Feet pushing
Fighting with the force of the wind
Stomach twisting and turning

Kids running
Splashing their tiny feet in the water
Giggling all over the place

Birds chirping
Leaves whistling in the breeze

The scent of red meat cooking on the grill

Sweet
Savory
Smoked
Honey

Oh, the summertime

Watermelon

Ice cream
Sweet tea

A Threesome. A Platonic Love Affair.

I don't think I'll ever want "a man."

I'm too busy having a huge fucking threesome.
A platonic love affair.

I have two of the most amazing men in my life
right now.

They love on my brain.
Embrace my body when it feels triumphant and
broken.
Hits all of my good spots…Guarding my fears from
the opposite sex.
Make me seek the depths of my own intellect daily.

They see me.
They get me.
They spend time with me.
They appreciate me.
They don't judge me.
They invest in me.
They support me.
They are consistent, persistent.

They value me.
They're resistant to my bullshit, an immovable force of comfort.

I catch myself calling you "girl" when we're communicating —
It's all just that deep and connective.

They remind me of my own view of myself and my reassurances.
They say I'm rare, a great mom, beautiful, and well deserving. Imperfectly polished and potent. A queen.

I'm smiling at how much I love and admire them.
They have no idea how fucking amazing they are either,
But I remind them as much as I possibly can.

Because they must know. They need to know that they are Kings!
Protectors.
Analytical perfectionists.
Driven goal warriors.
Selfless lovers.
Strong — mentally, physically.

Loving fathers and godfathers.
Perfectly imperfect.
Lovingly annoying.
(So annoying)
Forgiving.
Human.
With not one or two fucks to ever give to irrelevance.

These are only a few of the many ingredients to their inner armor.
They are so worth every single chance given —
I stay drilling that in their bricks for heads.

I dare a woman or man to try and taint that. Hurt them. They'll deal with me.
…I can be a bitch.

For someone to be broken in such a way at life-defining moments, it can be hard for one to open themselves back up, to heal from the neglect, hurt, and emptiness.

So, it's difficult for me to even have a minute interest in another romantically,
But these two came through with a force all their own

Like a swift, chilling, cool yet warming breeze
through a summer's sandy beach night.

Sitting beside me.
Wondering about me.
All inquisitive and legit and shit.
Needing and wanting to know more.
Holding my hand.
Patting and rubbing me on my back.
Backing me up.
Embracing my complexity and imperfections.
Seeing through all of the shaded, cracked screens.

And all I try to do is return it.
Because y'all deserve it,
And so much more…

Self-seeking? No.
Self-gratification? Of course not!
A love and connection in its purest, most innocent
form.

No orgasm needed.
Just the peace they bring to me.

Grace

My God!

Giving You the absolute best of me
The rawness of me
I can't back down
I must advance
Into Your place of glory
I am the only one capable

I'm after You!
My God!

I must release me
Relinquish me
So that I can gain You

You make me whole
No one loves me more than You

My God!

Wanting more?
Needing more?

Who I am? What I feel? What I think?

What I believe? What I see?

I give it all to You in exchange for grace and mercy

So that I may embody the very Spirit of thee

Without You I am absolutely nothing

My God!

Easy & Plain To See

You always saw the good
Great
Best
Worth

In Me

Never afraid to set me straight
Never afraid to love me and show it
Totally and completely deserving equally
I don't know how I was blessed with you

Loving you is as easy as breathing

Love strong

Love with pride

Let It Out

Last night I cried
My chest tight
Stinging
Wheezing
Breathing deep
Feeling my pain take over

Last night I cried
Over all the spilled milk
Over all the growing pains
Over all the trials and tribulations
Over all the love that I foolishly thought was mine

Last night I cried
Over my very existence
Over my unspoken worth
Over my lost life
Over my unheard dreams

Last night I cried
Over shoulda, coulda, woulda
Over the beginning, the middle and the end
(And can't forget those climaxes)

Last night I cried
Over guilt
Over sorrow
Over pain
Over abuse
Over worry —
All of the devil's seeds

Last night I cried

And prayed that Sweet Jesus take over before it takes
over me

Suppression

Suppressing your gift can control the quality and outcome of your life,

Make you doubt your purpose,

And keep the gifts that are only meant for you trapped.

The world is set up in such a way to make you do so.

So few takes the time to delve into their true selves anymore,

Sucked into what "average" is, acting accordingly.

Society shows you that success is only for those of privilege rather than an abundance of sheer, yet coarse, authenticity, grace and, god forbid…mercy.

Going against the grain isn't always bad.

Being the black sheep isn't always bad.

Being the result of generational curses isn't always bad, either.

Trust the gift and trust the process.

Love & Found

Stop trying to rationalize what kind of love you want and for once just let it happen.

Let love find you.

Love can never be found when its constantly chased — You may actually be running away from it.

Be still.
Be quiet.
Be humble.

Let God show you.

Faith

Strong
Tested
Concrete

I keep you safely lit in the darkest parts of my heart
You're the fuel to my life

My existence
My fight
My course

I'll never surrender to anything or anyone
But you…

You keep me sharp
You keep me focused

If I allow anything else into my life but you, I will
falter and question what's already certain

You

You're the reason for my beginning, middle, end

You're the reason for my reason

You're defiant in all seasons

The source of all things in life

So why question the question of your authority?

To go through, to get through and stay true is you

Unshaken
Unfathomable

You

A Mother's Love Note

My world
My joy
My reason for breathing

The sound of your heartbeat gave me life

Completion

I will do absolutely anything for you
To keep you safe
Healthy
Happy
Grounded

I'll never understand why I deserve you
I simply don't

God shows me His love through you

Because of you, I move forward
For you

So that you can grow in life, in love, in faith

To be better than me

G.O.A.T.

I don't want you.
I don't want it.
I just want me.
In my peace.

Let me go.
Let me breathe.

Release and vanquish the spell you have placed
upon me.

I won't allow you to smother me again.
Or devour me spirit whole.

I rebuke you — cast you out like a spell in the
presence of all that is beautiful, pure, right, inde-
pendent, and strong.

I've told you once
I'll tell you again —
I am the best at what I do.

The way that I use my words so eloquently and

delicately,
Elaborate on my inner most feeling,
Walk with my head high, back straight, with poise
and grace;

The way that I demonstrate and alleviate your pain,
Because I am much stronger than thee and desirable,
With enough courage to soothe your inner most
yearning for knowledge and thirst for my divine
flesh.

I can love, grow, teach, nurture, rectify, justify all
at once.
I can put you right in your place — Beside me,
amongst me,
Never above me.

You will not tell me what's right and wrong for me,
Proper and improper.

Open your eyes and take a look at my thick history.

I am your life line.
I am the best.

A WOMAN.

Now, bow down to me!

A Writer. A Poet.

Words are me.
I am words.

They come in different forms, different texts, different languages…and still have a way of being universal.

It is the most precise way in which I can share and relate myself to you.

They bring out this intense passion in me. This drive. This yearning. To speak in my own way. Create my own language.

For the touch of an incorrigible relation to and between words is so endearing.

Complacency

Don't ever get comfortable with anything or anyone
in this life

Because right now is all that you truly have

So don't waste it sitting
Simmering
Breathing that expensive, free flowing thing called
oxygen...
Eventually you won't be able to afford it

Seek more
Learn more
Embrace more
Do more
Feel more
Say more

Challenge it all

Two Is Better Than One

You lose folks when they're too much weight for you

Especially when they're lacking organic desire to be a part

Embrace those who want to share and lessen that weight

Those are the ones that matter

Prayer In Numbers

So throughout the day I prayed

For understanding
For clarity
For forgiveness
For salvation
For cleansing
For you

Shadowing

I wanted to take you with me
Allow you to see this part of me through your eyes
What I am
What I do
What I aspire to be
What I yearn for
Mostly what I want to escape from —
All of it is beautiful pain

If you could see the moon beyond the city lights
Tall structures of inorganic force, overly abundant,
and privileged living
Oh how I've longed to be amongst thee
Without losing my authenticity

Soul & Earth

Close your eyes
Kiss the sun
Bathe in the rain
Soak in the mud
Make love to the moon
Dream in the stars
Caress the grass
Grasp the wind
Soothe the ocean
Dance with the trees
Chase the snow
Brush the breeze
Tickle the sand
Clap with lightning
Embrace your body
Live with your soul

The Upside To Brokenness

Don't be a prisoner of your brokenness

Allow yourself to mend and balance

Heal and flourish into your righteous self

During this time, you may meet your soul partner

If this happens, don't rush it, push it, label it, manip-
ulate it, sexualize it (yes to no sex)…none of that!

Just relish in the process

Stay pure within yourself

And be open to the acceptance
Support
Love
Enhancement and encouragement you receive from
that soul partner

This will be a constant exchange between you two

They will understand, as it is a desire of two evenly
yolked souls

Peace

I want to rest in a home that's mine —
Open, clutter free
Fresh, modern, yet with history
With scents full of passion and happiness

I want smooth blankets on blades of grass
Bright starlit nights
Cups of hot tea
Pool illuminated by the moon and endless sky
As my kids rest in comfort, peace and happiness

I want to read
I want to write
I want to dance while listening to good music
As each nostalgic note possesses me, freeing me of
all inhibitions
Sending me into a trance of slow, flowing motions
only my heart can move to

I want bike rides
Oversized sun hats
Sundresses and sneakers
Shorts and long sleeves

Sun kissed skin
Steady beating hearts

I want to sit oceanside
Enveloped by the sound of its waves
Crisp, cool blankets and fresh fruits
The golden sun outlining the beauty of my son and
daughter
Their laughter joyous, carefree
We are thankful for mercy and grace
Change and balance
Calming our souls
Settling spirits
Rejuvenating my body

Dauntless

I am strength and confidence

I am love and light

I am absolute and certain

I am soulful and spiritual

I am wondrous and complex

I am the embodiment of resistance

I am loyal and passionate

I will survive this

My Orchid

I don't want you to do this alone

Mend those pieces
Break out of that darkness
Mold into your own
I need you
To come out here with me
Into the light
Into my arms
Embrace my heart

I know you've got questions
Fears
Worries
Doubts
But love I swear I'm all yours exclusively
You're the essence of my being

I know others said so and reneged
Touched your soul in the most private places
With false enlightenment and shaded sincerity
Bruising your heart
Tainting your spirit

Understand that you are
You are
You are light
An orchid upon its blooming
On the precipice of yet another life cycle
And that's okay
Because you're worth it

www.ingramcontent.com/pod-product-compliance
Lightning Source LLC
Chambersburg PA
CBHW071235090426
42736CB00014B/3098